TURKEY HUNTING

KATE CANINO

rosen publishing's
rosen central®

New York

This book is dedicated to Alex Wirth, an avid sharpshooter, who taught me how to shoot my first gun; Rob Elliott, whose bow hunting skills have always inspired me; and Chuck Cerankosky, who once said that "the only way to match the cunning of the elusive turkey is to study them, live amongst them, become one of them. Only then, after you have mastered an understanding of their every strut, every gobble, will they allow themselves to become your prey."

Published in 2011 by The Rosen Publishing Group, Inc.
29 East 21st Street, New York, NY 10010

First Edition

Library of Congress Cataloging-in-Publication Data

Canino, Kate.
Turkey hunting / Kate Canino.
    p. cm. — (Hunting: pursuing wild game!)
Includes bibliographical references and index.
ISBN 978-1-4488-1244-8 (library binding) —
ISBN 978-1-4488-2274-4 (pbk.) —
ISBN 978-1-4488-2277-5 (6-pack)
1. Turkey hunting—Juvenile literature. I. Title.
SK325.T8C25 2011
799.2'4645—dc22

                                                          2010018912

Manufactured in Malaysia

CPSIA Compliance Information: Batch #W11YA: For further information, contact Rosen Publishing, New York, New York, at 1-800-237-9932.

On the cover: Turkey hunting is a sport that is enjoyed by millions of people. This photo shows an Eastern wild turkey, the most commonly hunted species in the United States.

CONTENTS

People have hunted since the beginning of time. It was essential to the survival of early peoples, and it still is important in most cultures today. In North America, hunting is an activity that millions of people enjoy. People practice hunting for sport and as a way to provide food for themselves and their families.

Turkey hunting has grown in popularity over the years. According to Gary Clancy, author of *Wild Turkey*, more than four million sportsmen hunt turkeys each year. This book introduces many aspects of the sport of turkey hunting. Topics include firearms and archery safety, the behavior and habits of the turkey, and how to prepare for a hunt.

This book also explains how to attract the turkey and avoid spooking the bird. For example, you will learn what to wear while hunting in order to blend in with the surroundings. A hunter must wear the proper clothing to stay hidden. He or she must also remain completely silent: the wild turkey has extremely good sight and hearing. You will also learn the different calls that are used to bring a turkey in for the shot and what to do after the animal has been harvested.

Wildlife management and conservation is an extremely important aspect of turkey hunting. Without

Two hunters head home after a successful hunt near Sundance, Wyoming. Turkey hunting is a sport that can be enjoyed now and for generations to come.

programs to manage and protect wildlife, there might be no wild turkeys to hunt. Professionals in this field make sure the turkey population is protected and hunted responsibly. Hunters also have ethical and legal responsibilities that go along with hunting turkeys. This book will discuss some of the licensing fees and regulations that each hunter must follow in order to participate in turkey hunting legally.

If you are thinking about taking up the sport of turkey hunting, have a friend or family member that enjoys it, or have just started hunting, this book will begin your education in many of the areas a hunter needs to know about. Because of the rising popularity of turkey hunting, there are many informative Web sites, magazines, and books that you can read in conjunction with this book. In addition, seek out advice and help from experienced hunters to get the best and most up-to-date information for your area.

CHAPTER 1

INTRODUCTION TO TURKEY HUNTING

Many responsibilities come with hunting because firearms, live animals, and people are involved. Every state has its own regulations for both hunting and fishing. One needs to learn the local hunting regulations and what kind of turkey hunting is allowed in each season. Information can typically be found within a state's department of natural resources or department of game and wildlife. Wildlife is considered a publicly owned resource, and hunters must follow the proper rules and regulations for sharing and using this resource.

There are many Web sites that list the different hunting seasons for a chosen prey and that provide information about how to become a good hunter. When learning to hunt turkeys or any game animals, researching and using the proper gear and equipment is essential. One must develop persistence and patience, along

Turkey hunting can be a great way to create a tradition with family and friends. It can be enjoyed by different age groups and can be a terrific bonding experience.

with strong shooting skills, to become an accomplished hunter. Finally, it is important to understand that while the animal is the target, one must show respect for both the animal and nature.

Why People Choose to Hunt

People have many reasons for hunting. Some feel that it is a rite of passage that can significantly affect a person. They believe hunting can be a life-changing experience, giving young adults confidence and a sense of pride. Hunting can also be time well spent with family and friends. For many, getting together and going turkey hunting is a yearly tradition. John Ferguson, an expert turkey hunter in the New England area, says, "One of my most exciting hunts was taking my twelve-year-old niece out for her very first hunt. We didn't even hear a bird gobble the first day, but she shot her first tom at 8:30 AM the next morning. I think I was more excited than she was. It [hunting] provides great times and memories."

People also hunt for food. If a hunter is lucky enough to harvest the wild turkey, the prize is the meat that the animal offers. The wild game meat is much leaner than meat from farm-raised animals and is free of antibiotics and growth hormones. This is important to many people who are concerned about the source and quality of their food.

Some people hunt turkey for sport or for the challenge. Others see hunting as a stress reliever and a way to relax. Hunting can take one away from the busyness of life. When hunting turkeys, a person typically walks alone in the woods. He or she is forced to be as quiet as possible and just listen to the sounds of nature. In this serene environment, a person can be alone with one's thoughts. The sport also allows one to peek into the lives of wild animals and view them in their element.

National Wild Turkey Federation

The National Wild Turkey Federation (NWTF) has played a large role in managing the wild turkey population in the United States. This nonprofit conservation and hunting organization helps private landowners manage wildlife on their property. The organization uses licensing fees from hunters, along with fund-raising, to provide money to manage the turkey population. Some of the funds have been used for trap-and-release stocking programs. In these programs, turkeys are trapped in one place and then released in another place, where the turkey population is lower or the habitat is better suited to the birds.

When the NWTF was established in 1973, there were only 1.3 million wild turkeys. Today, that number stands at more than seven million birds throughout North America. Hunting seasons have been established in forty-nine U.S. states, Canada, and Mexico, thanks to the efforts of state, federal, and provincial wildlife agencies, as well as the NWTF and its partners. While wild turkey restoration is nearing completion, the NWTF still has much work to do. Across North America, supporters are working to enhance habitats for wild turkeys and other wildlife. At the same time, they are working to provide hunters with more opportunities and greater access to public and private land.

Students in Solon Springs, Wisconsin, release an Eastern wild turkey in an event with the National Wild Turkey Federation. Trap-and-release stocking programs have allowed the turkey population to thrive.

Wildlife Management

Wildlife management is a professional field in which people work to manage the wildlife in a certain area. Wildlife managers try to keep a population of wild animals, such as turkeys, at a desirable level. In their planning, managers must consider the capacity of the animal to reproduce and the factors that limit that capacity. Factors that limit a population's growth include loss of habitat, disease, predation, and hunter harvesting. Wildlife managers try to keep a balance between the factors that increase a population's growth and the factors that cut down a population's numbers.

Hunting in modern times is mainly for recreation, but it is also used to control the animal population. The different rules for the spring and fall hunting seasons are designed to help manage the wild turkey. During the spring hunting season, only toms (male turkeys) can be hunted. This helps ensure the survival of the hens (female turkeys) that are breeding. During the fall hunting season, a hunter is able to hunt both hens and toms. There are also the following limits to wild turkey hunting in many places:

1. Bag limits, or limits on the number of turkeys each hunter is able to harvest
2. Limits on shooting hours
3. Banning of certain weapons and ammunition
4. Restrictions on the use of decoys and blinds
5. Prohibitions on the use of electronic calls

It is important to understand the local hunting rules and regulations before going turkey hunting. Hunters should check the rules in their county, since the rules can vary from county to county.

Another part of wildlife management is managing land to improve wildlife habitats. By improving the land, wildlife managers create a place for turkeys and other wild animals to flourish, as well as a place for hunters to pass on their traditions.

Wildlife Conservation: Protecting Turkeys for the Future

Wildlife conservation is the act of protecting, preserving, and studying wildlife and wildlife resources. The U.S. Fish and Wildlife Service (FWS) reports that the primary source of funding for states' wildlife conservation efforts is the sale of hunting licenses, tags, and stamps. According to the bureau, when a hunter respects the hunting seasons, purchases all required licenses, and pays federal excise taxes on hunting equipment, the hunter helps ensure the future of many species and their habitats. The federal excise tax on hunting equipment raises about $200 million a year for conservation

A man enhances land for wild turkeys by planting foods such as wheat and clover.

programs. These programs benefit both hunted and nonhunted wild-life species.

Local hunting clubs and national conservation organizations also work to protect the future of wildlife. According to the FWS, such groups have set aside thousands of acres of habitat and have pushed for stronger conservation efforts in our national and state capitols. A number of interesting hunting clubs and conservation organizations are listed in the back of this book. An aspiring hunter can visit an organization's Web site, or become a member, to learn about hunting and how it affects the land and the extraordinary wildlife around us.

Hunters have a responsibility to treat game animals ethically and to take care of the land where the game lives. Being respectful to the turkeys and the land ensures that both will be conserved and will remain in a healthy state.

CHAPTER 2

ARCHERY AND FIREARM SAFETY

Before becoming a turkey hunter, it is important to become educated about firearms and/or archery, depending on what method one will use to hunt the turkey. If these tools are not used properly or responsibly, lives can be put in danger. As with any new hobby or skill, it takes practice and perseverance to become successful. Many professionals can show new hunters exactly how to use the tools necessary to hunt turkeys.

Firearm Safety

In order to handle a firearm safely, a person must respect the gun and treat every firearm as if it were loaded. One should never remove the safety on his or her gun until the turkey is positively identified. A hunter should never point a gun at anything he or she is not planning to shoot.

Any time firearms or weapons are involved in a sport, it is extremely important that one is trained to handle and use them. Safety should be the priority.

In addition, a hunter should not point a firearm in an unsafe direction, such as toward a person, a road, homes, or other buildings. Also, it is illegal for a person to discharge a firearm within 500 feet (152.4 meters) of any dwelling unless the hunter is the homeowner or has the owner's permission.

It is essential to know the location of one's target and what is behind the target. A missed shot from a shotgun can send stray ammunition traveling many yards beyond the intended target. Another rule is that a hunter should never shoot at a sound. One should always have a visual image and know exactly what he or she is shooting. If a person is not completely sure, he or she should not shoot.

Transporting and Carrying Firearms

A hunter needs to transport and carry a gun from his or her home to the hunting area. A number of states prohibit the carrying of uncased, loaded, long guns in a motor vehicle. Game wardens in many states strictly enforce regulations regarding the transportation of firearms during hunting season. As soon as any firearm (handgun, rifle, or shotgun) is carried on or about the person, or placed where it is readily accessible in a vehicle, state and local firearms laws regarding carrying apply. Some states have laws about carrying bows and crossbows as well. For up-to-date information on the laws and regulations in your state, visit the National Rifle Association's (NRA) Web site (http://www. nraila.org/GunLaws).

Shooting Training

In order to be a responsible hunter, a person must get proper training in handling his or her firearm, as well as a lot of practice shooting. If a person wants to learn how to shoot, he or she needs to understand

Target shooting is a great way to fine-tune the skills needed to hit a turkey. Practice will ensure a quick and successful harvest.

and practice the rules of firearms safety. When target shooting, always remember to wear both eye and ear protection. It is imperative to follow the rules of the range where one is practicing.

Target shooting is divided into three disciplines, according to the type of firearms used:

1. **Shotgun.** A semiautomatic or pump firearm for short-range shots
2. **Rifle.** A firearm designed to be fired from the shoulder
3. **Handgun.** A firearm designed to be held and operated using one hand

Introductory classes at the range will help you decide which shooting discipline and type of hunting action you like best. Beginners often enjoy developing skills in concentration, self-control, hand-eye coordination, and precision. Firing ranges have a variety of specially designed targets for practicing these skills. Some targets are moving and some are static, or still. Targets are also located at different distances.

Once you determine the disciplines and games you enjoy most, your local sporting goods retailer can help you gear up with the right equipment. In many places, turkey hunters are only allowed to shoot turkeys with a shotgun. Finding a firearm with the right fit, as well as one that is appropriate for turkey hunting, will make for a safer hunting experience. A knowledgeable retailer can also help a hunter find the right ammunition for the firearm. In addition, the retailer can direct a hunter to the correct safety equipment, including any mandatory eye and ear protection. The investment a hunter makes in equipment depends on how active or involved he or she wants to be.

More than nineteen million Americans safely participate in target shooting. The more target shooting an aspiring hunter does, the more prepared the person will be when he or she is hunting live turkeys out in the field.

Archery Equipment Safety

Some hunters enjoy using a bow and arrow when turkey hunting. The hunter must take good care of the archery equipment and handle it safely. By doing this, the hunter can ensure that everything works when it is time to hunt.

Just as when one is using a firearm, one should never point a bow at something that one is not targeting. A hunter should also never leave arrows on the string when he or she is not hunting or practicing.

Many turkey hunters choose to use a bow and arrow to harvest a turkey. If you are interested in archery, be sure to get the advice of a professional.

When transporting archery equipment, it is a good idea to keep the bow and arrows in an archery case. The case keeps the items from getting banged around when they are not in use. Don't leave an arrow knocked (set on the bowstring) when transporting the archery equipment. Before putting archery equipment away, make sure that any moisture has been properly wiped off the bow. Moisture can lead to rust. Also, use bowstring wax to keep the string in good shape when the equipment is not in use.

When carrying a bow, keep it at the side or in the front of the body to make sure it does not bang into anything. Doing this will prevent one from damaging the equipment and from making noise. If one's arm gets tired while carrying the bow, a bow handle strap can be used. This is strapped over the hand, allowing the hunter to relax his or her grip and hold the bow longer. A professional at an archery store can point out other handy tools that help hunters carry a bow for long periods of time.

Selecting a Shotgun

Due to turkey hunting's popularity, many new and improved shotguns have been designed specifically for turkey hunting. The following are some features to consider when selecting a shotgun and ammunition:

- Most turkey hunters hunt with a 12-gauge shotgun, which comes in a variety of different makes and models.
- A modern turkey shotgun often comes with a camouflage finish.
- A shotgun with a shorter barrel will be lighter and more maneuverable.
- A shotgun with a longer barrel allows the hunter to shoot at a greater distance from the target.
- Some shot sizes and shell lengths are unique to turkey hunting. The best ammunition delivers a dense, hard-hitting pattern at a distance of 40–45 yards (37–41 m).

Overall, the most important thing to consider when selecting a shotgun is whether the hunter can shoot it both comfortably and accurately.

Archery Training

A good bow hunter must practice, practice, practice! One should spend a lot of time learning how the bow works and using a target before going into the field. Taking a hunter safety course is an excellent way to learn archery basics. Many communities offer youth archery classes to make sure young people know the equipment and the rules.

When selecting a bow, make sure to choose one that is right for one's body size and strength. The weight of the bow (when the bow is drawn in) should be comfortable. In addition, many bows can be adjusted to a hunter's draw length. The draw length is the length of the string when it is pulled back. Everyone has a different draw length because everyone's arms are different sizes.

For advice on how to stand, how to hold your arms, and how to release the arrow, one should talk to an archery hunter. One important point to remember is this: stay relaxed. Being nervous will make the body jerk and interfere with one's ability to hit the target. Experienced hunters and archery teachers can work with you to fine-tune your abilities.

Bow Hunting vs. Firearms

According to John Ferguson, an avid turkey hunter from New England, some people believe it is easier to hunt with a gun than with a bow. However, regardless of which one you choose, you still need to be fairly close to your target. Ferguson says, "You must use a shotgun or bow, which limits your effective range to around 30 to 40 yards (27 to 36 m) depending on your abilities." It is very difficult to hunt turkeys with a bow without the use of a ground blind—a camouflage tent that covers the hunter. Turkeys see movement very well. Turkeys' eyes are on the sides of their heads, allowing them to see a full 360 degrees.

Rob Elliot, an avid bow hunter, says that he is licensed to hunt turkeys but has chosen not to because of their amazing eyesight. He said, "Many times when I have been bow hunting for deer, I have scared turkeys away—and I was hundreds of yards away from them! I figured out that I would need to become much better at being quiet in the woods before I would be up to the challenge of turkey hunting." All of the senses other than smell and taste are finely tuned in the turkey. If a turkey hunter's heart is set on using a bow and arrow, one must learn how to shoot accurately and move quietly.

Do Your Research

If a person wants to learn more about turkey hunting, there are many places to go to get reliable information without having to spend a lot of money. Most local libraries have books and magazines about hunting in general and turkey hunting specifically. It costs no money at all to get a library card. Internet research is also an excellent source of information. There are many sites about turkey hunting on the Web. Go online and see if there are any hunting safety courses in your area. A good place to look is wherever hunting licenses are purchased in your region. Also, talk to local hunters. They can give you a firsthand perspective on hunting wild turkey and tell you exactly what you need to do to prepare for hunting.

CHAPTER 3

HUNTER RESPONSIBILITIES AND PROFILE OF THE TURKEY

As a hunter of wild turkeys, there are certain laws and regulations one must follow. These laws are different in every state. Without laws and regulations in place, the turkey population, as well as the lives of hunters, would be put at risk. All hunters must understand their legal and ethical responsibilities in hunting the wild turkey. In addition, hunters must learn about the kinds of turkeys one may hunt and the areas in which one is allowed to hunt them.

Laws and Regulations

Most states require hunters to take courses in order to receive a license to hunt. For instance, in the state of New York, a ten-hour hunter education course is mandatory. In cases in which a person takes a course and

International Hunter Education Association

Continuing the heritage of hunting worldwide by developing safe, responsible and knowledgeable hunters.

Search

HOME   HUNTER EDUCATION   INSTRUCTORS   NEWS AND EVENTS   HUNTING AND SHOOTING   PARTNERS   ABOUT IHEA

International Hunter Education Association > Hunter Education

Hunter Education

http://wayneswicked.com/

Find a Course
OK. You are ready to sign up for a hunter education course, but you don't know how to find one. Start here!

Bowhunter Education Standards
Minimum standards for bowhunter education programs in North America.

Meet Our Students
Who takes hunter education courses, and what kinds of hunting do they do? Check out this page to see the adventures awaiting hunter education program graduates.

Hunter Education Requirements
Hunter education requirements vary by state. If you are planning a trip to another state or province, be sure to find out about the hunter education requirements. Don't lose your chance to hunt waiting until the last minute to find out the requirements.

Hunter Orange Requirements
Hunter orange clothing has saved many lives and lots of injuries. It works. Hunter orange regulations vary by jurisdiction, season, and game hunted. Theis page provides information from state and provincial wildlife agencies. Always check the annual regulations to be certain you are in compliance with current laws.

IHEA Clothing and Gear Store

IHEA Standards
The International Hunter Education Association has developed standards for hunter education in cooperation with IHEA partners and supporters.

Online Courses
Looking for an online hunter education course? Start here!

Replace Lost Cards
Millions of people have taken hunter education courses in North America. Each year a few people lose their cards. If you have lost your card, here are some tips and links to help you replace it.

Special offers for students
When a company or an organization makes us aware of special offers for hunter education students, we post the details here.

Become familiar with the hunting laws and requirements of your state before going out into the field to hunt turkeys. Many states require hunters to take a training course first.

then moves, some states will honor certificates and sporting licenses from other places. A special course may be required for those hunters who would like to bow hunt. In some states, children under the age of twelve cannot obtain a hunting license or hunt wildlife. Age restrictions vary from state to state.

There are different hunting seasons for different types of wild-life. Most states allow hunters to hunt wild turkeys in both the fall and the spring. However, there are often restrictions about the date ranges and areas in which you may hunt. Be sure to check date and area restrictions on the Web site of the local department of natural resources.

A hunter must have personal identification, such as a license, permit, tag, or stamp, which can only be used by the person to whom it is issued. Be sure to check that the license has all of the correct information, since any errors can make the license invalid. Some states require that back tags be visibly displayed in the middle of the back while hunting.

Ethics and Responsibilities

Turkey hunters have legal and ethical responsibilities when it comes to harvesting a wild turkey. A hunter must always respect the laws and regulations that have been enacted to protect the wild turkey and its habitat.

Legal hunting means that a hunter has the proper licenses and/or permits to hunt wild turkeys. As stated in chapter 1, the licensing fees for hunting help support wildlife conservation programs. Legally, one must show his or her license if a law enforcement officer or property owner demands to see it. It is illegal to use another person's license, permit, or stamp while hunting unless the person named on the license is present.

Having a license does not give the holder the right to go on a person's private property to hunt, unless he or she has the permission of the landowner. It is illegal to trespass on private property in order to hunt. One cannot enter or pass through the property without the agreement of the owner in writing.

Being an ethical hunter means respecting the animals one is hunting, as well as respecting nature and other hunters. One must follow the rules of fair chase and other hunting laws of the area. In addition, a hunter must be proficient with his or her weapon to ensure quick and clean kills. Further, if an animal is wounded, an ethical hunter will exhaust every means necessary to recover the animal.

According to John Ferguson, a responsible hunter does not take questionable shots. He or she must always be 100 percent sure of the target before pulling the trigger. Otherwise, unnecessary accidents can occur. The International Hunter Education Association Web site (http://www.ihea.com) gives current statistics on the number of hunting accidents that occur in the United States.

Many private landowners grant hunters permission to use their land. Others "post" their property, or mark it with a sign that says no hunting is allowed.

Hunting on Private and Public Land

Check the local department of natural resources or department of environmental conservation for hunting land locations and regulations for your state. There are many states that rely on private landowners for hunting and outdoor recreation. According to the New York State Department of Environmental Conservation (DEC), 85 percent of the state is privately owned, and many hunters practice the sport on private property. The department's Web site (http://www.dec.ny.gov) states, "Nearly two-thirds of the hunting in New York State is on private lands and more than 90 percent of all hunters will hunt on private lands during the hunting seasons."

The DEC gives a number of recommendations related to hunting on private land. First, as a responsible hunter, one must always seek permission prior to hunting on private land. This is true even if the land is not posted, or marked with a warning sign that says no hunting or trespassing. The DEC says that rural landowners are often willing to help hunters if hunters demonstrate courtesy to them and respect for their property. If, however, trespassing, littering, and vandalism occur, access will likely be denied to visitors. It is also important to note that disturbing any trees or plants on private land without the permission of the landowner is illegal. Finally, a hunter should always find a way to thank a landowner for granting permission to be on his or her land. For example, one could offer to share his or her game or to buy some of the landowner's crops.

Many states have public lands available for hunting and trapping during the appropriate seasons. To find information about the hunting opportunities and rules for public land, contact the regional office of the department of environmental conservation or department of natural resources for the county in which one desires to hunt. Staff can provide information about cooperative hunting areas and wildlife management areas. Some states require written permission or permits, which can be obtained from the regional office.

The Five Recognized Subspecies in North America

2009 Wild Turkey Ranges

- Eastern Wild Turkey
- Florida/Oceola Wild Turkey
- Gould's Wild Turkey
- Merriam's Wild Turkey
- Rio Grande Wild Turkey
- Hybrid Wild Turkey
- Ocellated Turkey (Central America)

0   110   220   440   660   880
Miles

This map shows where one can locate the five recognized turkey subspecies in North America. The Eastern wild turkey is the most widespread variety.

The Eastern turkey is the most abundant and widespread turkey species. There are more than five million of these birds inhabiting eastern, southern, and midwestern states, from Maine to Missouri. These turkeys live in diverse habitats such as forests in the Northeast, swamps in the South, and farmlands in the Midwest. The prime habitats for growing flocks are forests that are interspersed with fields, creeks, and rivers. The Eastern turkey roosts high up in the trees and across the flatlands. During poor weather, the turkeys seek warmth and shelter in evergreens. In the spring, gobblers (male turkeys) strut in open terrain, where hens are feeding and nesting.

The Osceola turkey range includes Florida, Georgia, and Louisiana. Osceola turkeys tend to roost in moss-laden cypress trees that grow in or on the edges of swamps, ponds, or creeks. During the fall, a hunter can find this species feeding in cattle pastures and burns. When springtime comes, these turkeys not only feed, but also strut and breed.

The Merriam's turkey is a species with approximately three hundred thousand to five hundred thousand birds. These turkeys inhabit fifteen Western states, including South Dakota, Idaho, and New Mexico. In Canada, the birds live in Manitoba and Alberta in small populations. Merriam's turkeys inhabit timbered prairies, grasslands, scrub-oak and pine foothills, and mountains. During the spring and summer, these birds live near snow-capped peaks. In the fall and winter, they migrate to lower elevations. Springtime means that gobblers are strutting for hens in mountain meadows or in grasslands near ponderosa pine roosts.

The Rio Grande turkey can be found in the South Central Plains. About one million Rios inhabit thirteen Plains and western states. Eighty-five percent of America's Rio Grande flock roams the Lone Star State, where they are dubbed Texas wild turkeys. Rio Grande turkeys typically roost in cottonwood, sycamore, and hackberry trees. Sometimes the turkeys will roost adjacent to grain fields, along streams, or in

The Rio Grande turkey is abundant in Texas and other states in the South Central Plains.

tall live oaks. In the fall, it is not uncommon to find one hundred or more birds packed into a single tight stand of big trees. In the spring, twenty or more longbearded toms, along with gaggles of hens and immature gobblers called jakes, might roost side by side in tall oaks

Turkey Behavior

Many people don't know that turkeys have excellent vision. They have the ability to twist their heads 360 degrees, so they can see all the way around. If you can see a turkey's head, the turkey can see you. A turkey's eyes are set in the sides of its head for monocular vision. Each eye is used separately, increasing the turkey's field of view. However, while turkeys see 20/20 during the day, they do have poor night vision. Turkeys also have extremely sharp hearing. This makes it hard for the hunter: the turkey can hear the slightest of sounds, from the slapping of brush to the clicking of the safety on a shotgun. This is because their ear flaps work to funnel in sound waves. On the other hand, turkeys are known to have a poor sense of smell. Also, turkeys are believed to have relatively few taste buds.

When a turkey senses that it is in danger, it will run with a tremendous amount of energy and quickness. The turkey will tuck its head low to the ground and tear off into the brush. Turkeys have strong, muscular legs, which are good for running and launching into the air. Turkeys are skittish creatures whose movements are unpredictable. Something as simple as the shadow of another animal is enough to spook, or scare, a turkey. These qualities make the turkey hunter's job a challenge.

Turkey hunters learn a great deal about turkey behavior and about the bird's physical strengths and weaknesses.

or cottonwoods. Male Rios strut all over their open habitat during the spring mating season. Many gobblers also like to stay in crop fields or pastures near creeks or other water sources. This is especially true if there are good hen-nesting habitats, with low brush or other horizontal cover, close by.

The Gould's turkey inhabits the mountains of northwestern Mexico. In addition, several hundred Gould's turkeys roam mountain ranges in southern Arizona and New Mexico. This turkey is known as a mountain bird, living in southwestern hills that range from 4,500 feet (1,372 m) to more than 7,000 feet (2,134 m) in elevation. The turkey's habitat is laced with steep, rough, and rocky canyons and drainages. Piñon pines and scrub oaks in the canyon bottoms provide Gould's turkeys with good food, roost trees, and nesting and security cover.

Some turkey hunters try to achieve the "grand slam" of turkey hunting. To do this, the hunter must harvest one of each of the five North American subspecies of turkey within a set period of time. Some try to reach this goal in one season or over a period of years.

CHAPTER 4

PLANNING THE HUNT

There are many things a turkey hunter needs to plan before the hunting season even begins, as well as just prior to the hunt. The hunter must consider many details, such as the places the local turkeys roost, what is best to wear out in the field, and how to call a turkey in for the shot. Turkeys are unpredictable birds that are easily spooked. They will run off if they see anything that is out of place, such as white socks peeking out from under a hunter's pants. The key to a successful hunt is to be fully prepared.

Prehunting Preparation

Scouting before hunting season means taking the time to see where the wild turkeys are gathering. This is important preparation for the actual hunt: a hunter will be much more efficient with information about where

Scouting for evidence of turkeys, including tracks, scratches, droppings, and feathers, lets hunters know where the turkeys tend to gather.

the turkeys are spending time. One should hike around the hunt zones a month or so before the season starts.

When scouting, look for tracks and scats (droppings). There is a noticeable difference in the appearance of a hen's and a gobbler's tracks and scats. Checking local library resources and going online are great ways to research turkey tracks and scats. Also, as opening day approaches, walk or drive around and listen for gobbles. Mark the areas where you hear the sounds on a map to remember where to go when it is time to hunt.

Listening and Calling the Turkey

When listening for the wild turkey, it is important to know that different turkeys make different sounds. An excited hen makes a series of fast, loud, erratic single notes: this is known as cutting. On the other hand, a typical gobble from a gobbler or tom lasts for as long as two to three seconds. An older tom will have a deep, full-throated gobble. A jake, or young male, has a shorter gobble. Wild turkeys are very vocal in the late winter and early spring. A hunter will hear yelping, cutting, gobbling, purring, and other sounds.

The Web site of the National Wildlife Federation (http://www.nwf. org) is just one of the many sites that allow hunters to listen to the different turkey sounds and become familiar with them. Then, when hunting, the noises will be recognizable. Hunters use turkey calls to simulate the different sounds and draw in wild turkeys. For example, a hunter can make the noises a hen makes to attract a tom.

Once a hunter gets a tom to gobble, he or she shouldn't overcall the turkey, or bother it with too many calls. One should let the tom gobble a few times between calls because the tom is trying to call the hen (who is really the hunter). If the tom stops gobbling, the hunter should stop calling altogether. This may make the turkey come to look for him

The instruments above, known as box calls, are used to produce turkey sounds. There are many different calls that hunters can use to lure turkeys.

or her. Sometimes a tom will gobble a few times and then approach silently. A hunter should be patient and shouldn't give up too early on a bird. A lack of gobbling does not necessarily mean the tom is not coming. Sometimes it helps to use a decoy to direct the turkey's attention elsewhere. When the hunter is ready to shoot, he or she can remove the safety on the weapon and fire.

The National Wild Turkey Federation Web site (http://www.nwtf. org) is another place to listen to each of the different turkey calls. Here are just a few of the sounds that wild turkeys make:

- **Cluck.** One or more short, staccato notes, usually used by one bird to get the attention of another.
- **Putt.** This sound signals danger to other birds. It indicates that a turkey has seen or heard something that it doesn't like. It can be a single note or several sharp, rapid notes.
- **Tree call.** A series of soft, muffled yelps made by a roosted bird. It is used as a way to communicate with others in the flock.
- **Gobble.** This sound is made by the male wild turkey. It is primarily used during the springtime to let hens know he is in the vicinity.
- **Yelp.** A series of single-note vocalizations. A yelp can have different meanings, depending on the way the turkey uses it.

It is helpful to be familiar with a variety of turkey calls. Using just one of these calls may not always work to draw in a turkey. The more calls you know, the better you will be at hunting. Here are some examples of turkey calls that hunters use:

- **Diaphragm call.** This air-activated device consists of latex reeds, an aluminum frame, and a skirt. One makes turkey sounds by pushing air through the call and forming the mouth to say certain words. This is the most popular call, but the hardest to master.

- **Slate Call.** To make sounds, a hunter pulls a striker across a circular surface that is made out of slate, glass, aluminum, or a combination of these materials. Most beginners can pick up this call very quickly.
- **Box Call.** A hunter simply slides a wooden lid across an open box to create the sound. This is one of the easiest calls to learn.

Spring Turkey Hunting vs. Fall Turkey Hunting

According to John Ferguson, spring turkey hunting is exciting, challenging, and fast paced. In springtime, hunters can harvest only toms. To call in a male, or "tom turkey," hunters need to mimic hens because

A hen roosts with its poults (young turkeys) on a spring night. In springtime, a hunter is permitted to hunt only the tom, or male turkey.

this is the breeding season. This is achieved by using diaphragm calls, slate calls, or wooden box calls. It takes practice to become proficient with these calls. One wrong sound can be the difference between harvesting a turkey and going home empty-handed. It is possible to call a tom from more than half a mile (805 m) away. Sometimes a bird will come in within a few minutes. Other times a hunter will have to work with a turkey for hours.

During the fall hunting season, a hunter is allowed to take either male or female turkeys. The key is to try to ambush the birds at their food sources. Turkeys are only concerned with feeding and staying alive in the fall, so food sources and roosting areas (sleeping areas) are the best places to scout. If a hunter scatters a flock in the fall, he or she can usually use soft clucks to bring the birds back in. A hunter is not able to shoot a turkey that is in roost, but must wait until the turkey is on the ground.

Physical Condition of the Hunter

When preparing for turkey hunting, one must not only have the proper training and equipment, but must also be in good physical condition. There are many ways a person can prepare for the physical demands of hunting. For example, one can exercise on a daily basis and practice healthy eating habits.

It is also important for a hunter to be aware of his or her physical limitations. Many hunting injuries or deaths come from hunters having heart attacks or suffering heatstroke because they were not used to the physical exertion of hunting. This usually occurs more frequently in older adults. However, as a young hunter, it is a good idea to get in shape now and build healthy habits. Some hunters wisely spend a few weeks before hunting season in the gym or outdoors, building up their endurance and strength.

During the fall hunting season, hunters may harvest both the female turkey *(left)* and the male turkey *(right)*.

Personal Safety and the Safety of Others

When turkey hunting, there is a proper way for a hunter to sit and wait for a turkey. The guidelines include the following rules: First, the hunter should not load the gun until he or she is set up and calling the turkey in. Whenever you can hear another hunter working a bird, do not go in that area at all. If you are not completely sure that you are the only one working a bird, do not take any chances. It is never worth taking a risk if you or someone else might get hurt.

Yelping while on the move in the woods can be detrimental. Another hunter may hear the sound and mistake it for a wild turkey. His or her adrenaline can kick in and lead to an accident. Sit still and spend some time really observing your surroundings and listening for signs of hunters. Before raising a gun or bow, be absolutely sure that it is a turkey you are hunting and not another person. If another hunter is visible, let him or her know by shouting a loud and firm "Good morning!" or by saying, "It's a beautiful day out!" Wait to show yourself until the other person's gun is down and he or she is relaxed. After shooting a turkey, place it in an orange vest or carrying bag so that other hunters see a bag and not a wild turkey moving.

Hunting Clothing

As a hunter, one needs to be concerned about camouflage as well as comfort, silence, safety, and warmth. Expert turkey hunter Ben Cowan says that he lives by two clothing rules when hunting in the woods: First, purchase quiet fabric that provides comfort from the elements and mosquitoes. Second, remember to think about everything from your undergarments to pieces that will cover you from head to toe.

What to Bring on the Hunt

The following is a packing list of items to bring along on a turkey hunt:

1. Bug repellant
2. Call-tuning kit
3. Compact binoculars
4. GPS
5. Cushion
6. Extra shells
7. First-aid kit
8. Flashlight
9. Knife/multitool
10. Orange cap (for after the shot)
11. Pocket camera
12. Water and snacks
13. Rain gear
14. Warm hat
15. Gun or bow
16. Hunting license

A hunter's undergarments should be made from modern synthetic fabrics, which wick away moisture and keep a hunter warm. Purchasing green, brown, or camouflage long johns will ensure that no light colors pop out from underneath clothing. For outerwear, a hunter should wear full camouflage, including coverage for the hands and face. Turkeys have excellent vision. Pants should have enough length so that the legs are covered when one is sitting with the knees drawn up.

Many hunters consider a vest the most important article of clothing because it works like both a suitcase and a filing cabinet. It provides storage for calls and other various tools needed while hunting. Some vests have a cushioned seat attached for comfort when the hunter has to sit for long periods of time.

Head and face coverings are also key items. A hunter should wear a mask so that he or she will not expose a shiny forehead or rosy cheeks.

Wearing appropriate clothing is essential for a successful harvest. The hunter must be completely camouflaged and wear clothes that make no noise when one is moving.

Wild turkeys will pick up on such details with their keen eyesight. When the weather is hot, one can wear a mesh camouflage baseball cap. Gloves should also be camouflage and have long, knit wrists. Make sure that the gloves are thin: the hunter's hands should be unobstructed so that he or she can give calls, release the safety on a gun, pull a trigger, or shoot a bow.

A turkey hunter's footwear depends on the season. Tall rubber boots with good cushioning and foot support are great for rainy weather. Insulated leather boots work well when the weather is cold. Good, waterproof hiking boots can also keep the feet warm. A thin pair of polypropylene liner socks combined with wool outer socks will help wick away moisture and keep the feet dry and comfortable.

CHAPTER 5

HUNTING STRATEGIES AND TECHNIQUES

There are a variety of strategies and techniques that a good hunter can use, depending on the season and the weather. There are also different techniques to use when hunting alone or with a group. When a turkey is harvested, the hunter needs to know how to prepare the turkey to be brought off the field. The hunter also needs to decide whether he or she will mount the prized turkey as a trophy for friends and family to see. Hunting turkeys involves a lot of time, preparation, and physical endurance. The more strategies and techniques a hunter has for calling in a turkey, the better the hunting experience will be.

Still-Hunting

Still-hunting involves slowly and quietly stalking an animal. The best time to use this hunting tactic is when the weather is rainy and the ground is wet and soft. The moist land absorbs the sound of footsteps, allowing the hunter to stalk in a quiet fashion. According to the Web site Deer and Turkey Hunting Tips (http://www.warrior-critic.com), "The best technique for still-hunting is to move slowly and methodically throughout the woods. Walk short distances as quietly as possible. Stop and look around the area thoroughly before moving on." Excess movement is not recommended. A person's movements will spook the bird and send it running in the other direction.

Hunting with a Team

Group hunts can be fun because it is time spent with others doing an activity everyone enjoys. It is also an opportunity to learn from others

Hunting with a family member or friend can be an enjoyable experience. In group hunting, partners can cooperate and learn from one another.

with more experience or teach someone who is new to the sport. Hunters should always hunt with compatible partners. One can choose someone who has the same hunting style or someone who knows techniques that he or she would like to learn.

Choose one person to be in charge of the hunt so that there is no confusion when everyone is out in the field. Always be aware of your hunting partners' locations. Also, be sure to establish silent hand signals before the hunt. Any talking in the woods will scare the turkeys.

Hunting in Bad Weather

Hunting seasons cannot be extended due to bad weather. In order to make the best use of the available time, it is important to know what to do when conditions are not ideal.

When there is a lot of wind, it is very difficult to hear a turkey approaching. As a turkey hunter, one relies on close listening in order to locate the turkey. Find places with less wind, like valleys or the sides of a hill, which give some protection. Allow the wind to be at your back. That way, the wind will carry the sounds of the turkey to you.

In rainy conditions, turkeys are still active, even though the sun is not shining. The problem is that one cannot hear the hunter's call—or the turkeys'—as well above the sound of the rain. Keep in mind that turkeys usually start gobbling right before and after a storm. During the rain and just after it has stopped, turkeys will often go out into the open fields. There, they can see more clearly, which helps protect them from sneaky predators. Make sure the proper rain gear is close at hand. Otherwise, the rain could make for a miserable outing.

In snowy weather, a hunter must wear the proper attire. Realize your limitations, and don't allow frostbite to develop. Always be sure that the campsite is close enough so that you will be able to make it back to your truck and/or camp. Turkeys may be quieter when there is

Turkeys can be harvested even in inclement weather. For a safe and comfortable hunting experience, be prepared with the proper attire.

snow, but against the white background, they are more visible to the hunter's eye.

Part of being a responsible hunter is being prepared for everything. Check the local forecast on television, the radio, or online. It is better for the hunter to be overprepared than to lack items he or she needs. Layers can always be removed and stored at the campsite or in the truck.

Group Hunting Tactics

Hunting with others can be enjoyable, especially when your efforts lead to success. The following are some strategies to try when hunting with a group:

- Split up well before sunrise to listen in different locations for gobbles. Then meet up several minutes before sunrise to compare notes.

- One person can "yelp," while the other stays still and listens.

- Set up and work a gobbler side by side. Whisper to communicate with each other.

- Set up a system of nonverbal communication. Use hand signals or read one another's body language.

Taking the Shot

When setting up to shoot a turkey, do not attempt to get close to the roost. Patience is key. A hunter needs to sit still and quietly wait for the approaching bird. A responsible and ethical hunter will wait to take the right shot so that the bird is cleanly harvested. When one spots the red, white, and blue head and the swinging beard of the turkey within about 40 yards (36 m), it is time to take the shot. A hunter using a shotgun looks behind the turkey for safety, waits for the turkey to extend its neck, and then shoots the base of the neck. A hunter using a bow aims for the body of the bird.

Shotgun

Bow

When harvesting a bird with a shotgun or bow, an ethical hunter tries to get a clean shot in the proper location.

After the Hunt

After a hunter has harvested a turkey, steps must be taken to ensure the proper preservation of the bird and the ability to safely consume the meat. In order to field dress a turkey (one that will not be made into a full-size mount), the hunter places the turkey on its back wings. He or she moves the wings to the sides and points the legs up. The hunter inserts the tip of a knife at the bottom of the breastplate and cuts back to the anal vent. One proceeds to remove all of the entrails through this opening. Then, one removes the heart and lungs by reaching up into the cavity to sever the windpipe. The hunter uses a damp

In order to enjoy one's prized turkeys, it is important to field dress and transport them correctly after they are harvested.

paper towel to clean blood from the feathers if he or she plans to have the bird mounted.

After the turkey has been field dressed, the hunter tucks the prized turkey into a vest or carries it by the legs, not the neck. One must carry the bird with care, especially if it is going to be preserved by a taxidermist. The hunter wraps an orange vest or an orange bag around the bird until it is placed in the vehicle. That way, another hunter won't mistake it for a live bird. One should put the bird on ice to keep it cool while transporting it. If the hunter is not able to get the turkey to a taxidermist right away, the bird should be frozen.

The next step is to skin the turkey. First, the hunter cuts through the skin from the chest to the anal vent. Starting at the neck, the hunter skins the bird, cutting the neck bone and flesh without cutting through the neck skin. The head remains attached to the neck skin, which remains attached to the body skin. The hunter proceeds to skin down the back of the bird toward the wings and legs. One dislocates the wing bone from the body. Then one works down to the legs and dislocates each leg from the body. The bones and the wings are left intact. The hunter disconnects the tail from the body but leaves the tail attached to the skin. Then one completely skins the back of the bird. One also tries to gently remove any blood from the feathers.

Taxidermy

Taxidermy is a term for the variety of methods used to reproduce a lifelike, three-dimensional representation of an animal. A turkey hunter goes to a taxidermist so that the harvested turkey can be put on permanent display. There are many ways that a hunter can have the turkey displayed.

A life-size mount can be made in any position a hunter can imagine. In the most popular pose, a tom looks like it is gobbling on the

If you want a harvested turkey to become a showpiece in your home, take it to a taxidermist. There are many different ways to showcase a turkey.

roost while it hangs on the wall. Other options are the strutting pose or the standing pose. Another possibility is to do a half-mount using just the chest, head, and fan of the bird. Taxidermists mount the turkey by taking the skin and slipping it over a foam-plastic body. A newer option is to place an artificial head and chest in front of the natural tail fanning out on a plaque.

Turkey hunting is a sport that one should pursue with a lot of thought and research. A great deal of work goes into preparing for the hunt. A hunter can feel a great sense of pride and fulfillment when he or she carries the turkey home to be eaten and mounted. As a young adult, turkey hunting is a great way to learn patience and endurance and to gain a greater respect for nature.

Here are some final pieces of advice: Find hunting companions who are enthusiastic and have a lot of experience. Learning from the best will make a person a better hunter. Be sure to always practice safe hunting techniques, and value the whole experience of the hunt, not just the shot. Hunting ethically and responsibly will ensure a positive and safe experience, not only for the hunter, but also for the wild turkey.

GLOSSARY

blind A hiding place, similar to a tent, which is used by hunters.

breed To produce offspring.

decoy Something used to lure game into a trap or within gunshot.

field dressing Preparing the harvested animal for further use, primarily by removing the internal organs.

game Wild animals hunted for sport or food.

game warden An official who manages game animals or wildlife.

gobbler A male turkey.

habitat The surroundings and/or natural conditions in which a plant or animal lives.

harvest To shoot, trap, or catch fish or game.

hen A female turkey.

hunting season The season during which people are legally permitted to hunt a particular species.

jake An immature male turkey.

mandatory Something required or commanded by authority.

monocular vision A kind of vision in which each eye is used separately.

predation The act of seizing and feeding upon prey.

roost A place where a winged animal rests and sleeps.

scats Fecal droppings of an animal.

scout To explore in order to gain information.

taxidermist A person who specializes in stuffing and mounting the skins of animals for display.

tom A male turkey.

tracks Marks or other discoverable evidence left by an animal.

wildlife conservation The planned protection, preservation, and study of wildlife and wildlife resources.

wildlife management The act of managing a population of animals.

Canadian Shooting Sports Association (CSSA)

7 Director Court, Unit #106

Vaughan, ON L4L 4S5

Canada

(905) 265-0692

Web site: http://www.cdnshootingsports.org

The CSSA is the voice of amateur shooting and firearms enthusiasts in Canada. The organization supports and promotes all kinds of shooting sports, including hunting and archery. The CSSA is politically active in fighting for the rights of responsible Canadians to have lawful access to firearms.

National Rifle Association (NRA)

11250 Waples Mill Road

Fairfax, VA 22030

(800) 672-3888

Web site: http://www.nra.org

The NRA has been a leader in firearms education in the United States since its founding in 1871. The organization provides publications and pro-gramming for youth with an interest in hunting. The NRA relies on the efforts and service of its approximately four million members.

National Shooting Sports Foundation (NSSF)

Flintlock Ridge Office Center

11 Mile Hill Road

Newtown, CT 06470-2359

(203) 426-1320

Web site: http://www.nssf.org

The NSSF is the trade association for the shooting, hunting, and firearms industry. Formed in 1961, the NSSF is a nonprofit organization that promotes, protects, and preserves hunting and the shooting sports.

National Wild Turkey Federation

P.O. Box 530

Edgefield, SC 29824-0530

(800) 843-6983

Web site: http://www.nwtf.org

The National Wild Turkey Federation is a national nonprofit conservation and hunting organization that, along with its volunteers, partners, and sponsors, works for the conservation and preservation of the wild turkey.

Professional Bowhunters Society

P.O. Box 246

Terrell, NC 28682

(704) 664-2534

Web site: http://www.probowsociety.org

The Professional Bowhunters Society has been a strong force in the promotion of bowhunting. It is an organization of experienced bowhunters who value leadership and knowledge through experience.

Web Sites

Due to the changing nature of Internet links, Rosen Publishing has developed an online list of Web sites related to the subject of this book. This site is updated regularly. Please use this link to access the list:

http://www.rosenlinks.com/hunt/turk

Casada, James A., ed. *America's Greatest Game Bird: Archibald Rutledge's Turkey-Hunting Tales*. Columbia, SC: University of South Carolina Press, 1994.

Combs, Richard P. *Guide to Advanced Turkey Hunting* (Outdoorsman's Edge Guides). Upper Saddle River, NJ: Creative Outdoors, 2004.

Gaetz, Dayle Campbell. *Crossbow* (Orca Currents). Victoria, BC, Canada: Orca Book Publishers, 2007.

Hickoff, Steve. *Fall and Winter Turkey Hunter's Handbook*. Mechanicsburg, PA: Stackpole Books, 2007.

Hickoff, Steve. *Turkey Calls and Calling: Guide to Improving Your Turkey-Talking Skills*. Mechanicsburg, PA: Stackpole Books, 2009.

Humphrey, Bob. *Turkey Hunting: Use the Secrets of the Pros to Bag More Birds* (Pro Tactics). Guilford, CT: Lyons Press, 2009.

Hutto, Joe. *Illumination in the Flatwoods: A Season with the Wild Turkey*. Guilford, CT: Lyons Press, 2006.

Kelly, Tom. *Tenth Legion: Tips, Tactics, and Insights on Turkey Hunting*. Guilford, CT: Lyons Press, 2005.

Lewis, Russell E. *The Art of American Game Calls: Duck, Goose, Turkey, and More: Identification and Values*. Paducah, KY: Collector Books, 2005.

Lovett, Brian. *Hunting Tough Turkeys*. Mechanicsburg, PA: Stackpole Books, 2010.

MacRae, Sloan. *Turkey Hunting*. New York, NY: PowerKids Press, 2011.

McIlhenny, Edward Avery, Charles L. Jordan, and Robert Wilson Shufeldt. *The Wild Turkey and Its Hunting*. Charleston, SC: BiblioLife, 2009.

Phillips, John. *Secrets of Successful Turkey Hunting* (Outdoor Classics). Chaska, MN: Publishing Solutions LLC, 2003.

Scheer, Julian. *A Thanksgiving Turkey*. New York, NY: Holiday House, 2001.

BIBLIOGRAPHY

Bourjaily, Philip. *The Field & Stream Turkey Hunting Handbook* (Field & Stream Fishing and Hunting Library). New York, NY: Lyons Press, 1999.

Clancy, Gary. *Wild Turkey* (Complete Hunter). Minnetonka, MN: Cowles, 1996.

Deer and Turkey Hunting Tips. "Turkey Facts." 2010. Retrieved March 2, 2010 (http://warriorcritic.com/turkey-facts).

Elliot, Robert. E-mail interview with author, January 17, 2010.

Eye, Ray. *Practical Turkey Hunting Strategies: How to Effectively Hunt Birds Under Any Conditions*. Guilford, CT: Lyons Press, 2003.

Ferguson, John. E-mail interview with author, January 15, 2010.

Hanback, Michael. *Advanced Turkey Hunting* (Complete Hunter). Chanhassen, MN: Creative Publishing, 2003.

HuntersAlley.com. "Hunting Tips for Becoming an Expert Animal Hunter." 2009. Retrieved March 3, 2010 (http://www.huntersalley.com/hunting_tips).

HuntingNet.com. "Turkey History." 2007. Retrieved March 3, 2010 (http://www.huntingnet.com/staticpages/staticpage_detail.aspx?id=192).

HuntingNet.com. "Turkey Hunting—Safety." Retrieved March 9, 2010 (http://www.huntingnet.com/staticpages/staticpage_detail.aspx?id=211).

Mettler, John J. *Wild Turkeys: Hunting and Watching*. Pownal, VT: Storey Books, 1998.

National Shooting Sports Foundation. "Get Started in Shooting." Retrieved March 12, 2010 (http://huntandshoot.org/Get_Started_Shooting.cfm).

New York State Department of Environmental Conservation. "Places to Hunt in New York." Retrieved March 15, 2010 (http://www.dec.ny.gov/outdoor/7844.html).

Ramsdale, Robert. "Hunting Tips." The Wild Turkey Zone, 2006. Retrieved March 2, 2010 (http://www.wildturkeyzone.com/hunting/tips.htm).

Sapir, Glenn. *Hunt Wild Turkey! Pros' Secrets for Success*. Minnetonka, MN: Shady Oak Press, 2008.

Trout, John. *The Complete Book of Wild Turkey Hunting: A Handbook of Techniques and Strategies*. New York, NY: Lyons Press, 2000.

TurkeyHunting.com. "History of the American Wild Turkey." Retrieved March 12, 2010 (http://www.turkeyhunting.com/content/general-information/turkey-history.aspx).

U.S. Fish and Wildlife Service. "USFWS—Hunting." 2010. Retrieved February 5, 2010 (http://www.fws.gov/hunting).

U.S. Fish and Wildlife Service. "What Do Hunters Do for Conservation?" December 12, 2007. Retrieved February 15, 2010 (http://www.fws.gov/hunting/whatdo.html).

INDEX

About the Author

Kate Canino is an author and educator currently living in Rochester, New York. A graduate of the College of Saint Rose in childhood education, she is always trying to inspire kids to educate themselves and become active in hobbies they are interested in. She has many friends who enjoy turkey hunting, bowhunting, and target shooting and loves to hear their stories about what it is like to be out in the wilderness. She has two books published by Rosen Publishing, one on the health benefits of cycling for kids and the other on controlling weight and building healthy habits.

About the Consultant

Benjamin Cowan has over twenty years of both big game and small game hunting experience. In addition to being an avid hunter, Mr. Cowan is also a member of many conservation organizations. He currently resides in west Tennessee.

Photo Credits